Number fun

PRICE STERN SLOAN LIMITED, NORTHAMPTON, ENGLAND

Questron®

The fun way to bring learning to life

This book is part of the **Questron** system, which offers children a unique aid to learning and endless hours of challenging entertainment.

The **Questron** Electronic Answer Wand uses a microchip to sense correct and incorrect answers with "right" or "wrong" sounds and lights. Victory sounds and lights reward the user when particular sets of questions or games are completed. Powered by a nine-volt alkaline battery, which is activated only when the wand is pressed on a page, **Questron** should have an exceptionally long life. The **Questron** Electronic Answer Wand can be used with any book in the **Questron** series.

A note to parents...

With **Questron**, right or wrong answers are indicated instantly and can be tried over and over again to reinforce learning and improve skills. Children need not be restricted to the books designated for their age group, as interests and rates of development vary widely. Also, within many of the books, certain pages are designed for the older end of the age group and will provide a stimulating challenge to younger children.

Many activities are designed at different levels. For example, the child can select an answer by recognizing a letter or by reading an entire word. The activities for pre-readers and early readers are intended to be used with parental assistance. Interaction with parents or older children will stimulate the learning experience.

Printed in Great Britain by
Purnell Book Production Limited
Member of the BPCC Group

How to start
Questron®

Hold **Questron**
at this angle and press the
activator button firmly on the page.

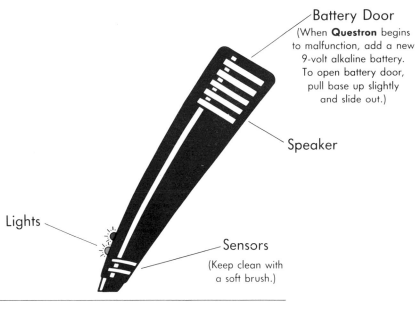

Battery Door
(When **Questron** begins
to malfunction, add a new
9-volt alkaline battery.
To open battery door,
pull base up slightly
and slide out.)

Speaker

Lights

Sensors
(Keep clean with
a soft brush.)

How to use
Questron®

Press
Press **Questron** firmly on
the shape below, then lift it off.

Track
Press **Questron** down on "Start" and keep it
pressed down as you move to "Finish".

Start

Finish

Right and wrong with
Questron®

Press **Questron**
on the square.

Press **Questron**
on the triangle.

Press **Questron**
on the circle.

See the green light and
hear the sound. This
green light and sound
say "You are correct".

The red light and sound
say "Try again". Lift
Questron off the page and
wait for the sound to stop.

Hear the victory sound.
Don't be dazzled
by the flashing lights.
You deserve them.

How Many Do You See?

Press **QUESTRON** on the square that has the correct answer to each question.

How many presents?

How many balloons?

How many bottles of pop?

How many hats?

How many candles?

How many ice creams?

How many plates in the stack?

How many noisemakers?

Snow, Sledges, and Scarves

How many are there in each box?
Track **QUESTRON** on the letters
that spell the name of each number.

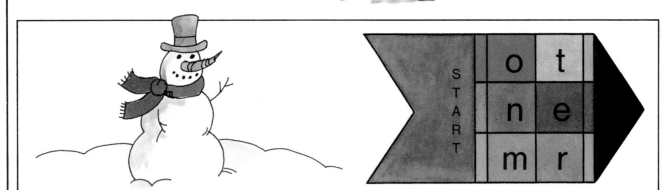

	o	t
START	n	e
	m	r

	t	p
START	w	o
	e	t

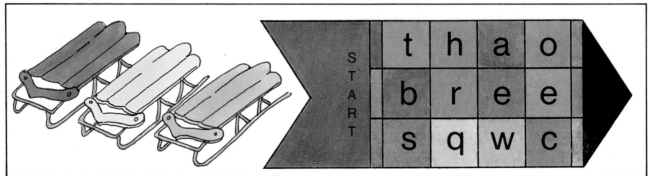

	t	h	a	o
START	b	r	e	e
	s	q	w	c

	f	i	v
START	o	u	r
	t	s	d

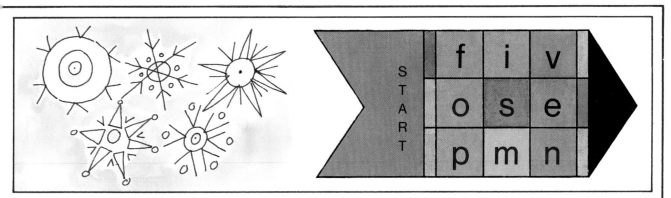

START

f	i	v
o	s	e
p	m	n

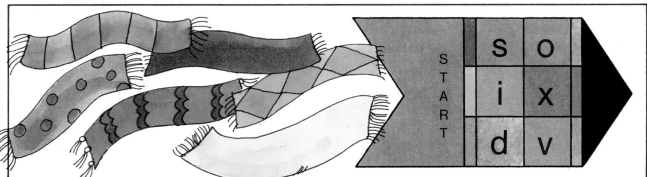

START

s	o
i	x
d	v

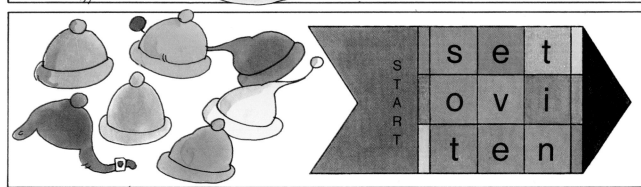

START

s	e	t
o	v	i
t	e	n

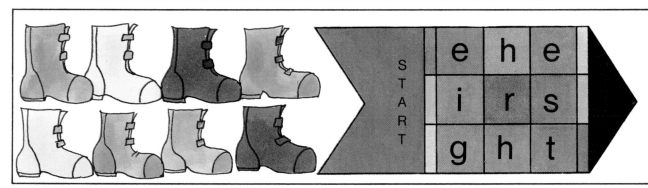

START

e	h	e
i	r	s
g	h	t

START

n	i	n
e	m	e
o	p	o

7

How Many Pets?

Add the numbers in each box to see how many animals are for sale. Press **QUESTRON** on each correct answer.

2+3

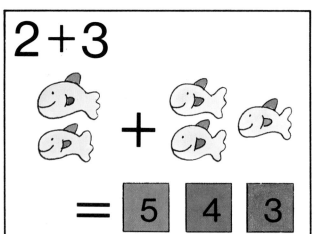

= | 5 | 4 | 3 |

2+4

= | 6 | 7 | 8 |

2+5

= | 6 | 7 | 8 |

2+1

= | 4 | 3 | 2 |

8

3+4

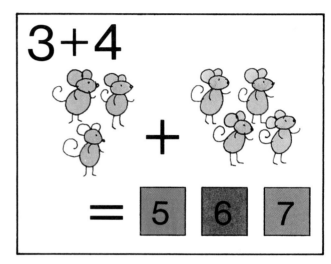

= 5 6 7

6+4

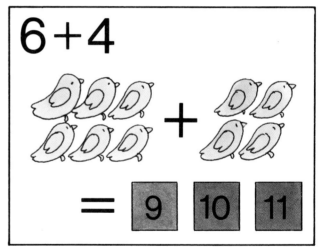

= 9 10 11

4+4

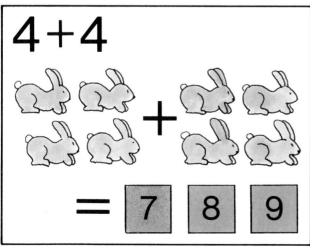

= 7 8 9

3+3

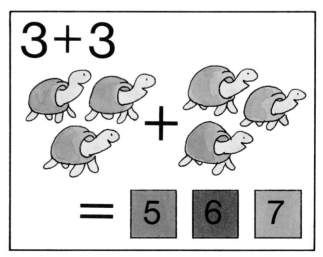

= 5 6 7

5−2

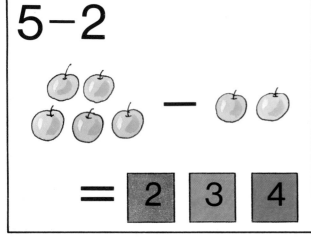

= 2 | 3 | 4

8−4

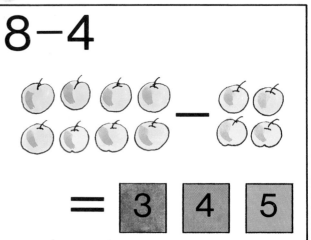

= 3 | 4 | 5

4−3

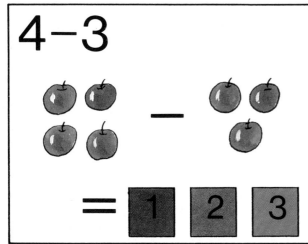

= 1 | 2 | 3

6−4

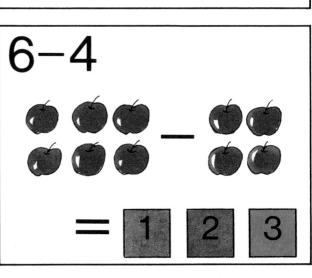

= 1 | 2 | 3

Bushels of Fun!

Subtract the numbers in each box
to find out how many apples are left.
Press **QUESTRON** on the correct answers.

6−3

= 3 4 5

5−1

= 2 3 4

3−2

= 1 2 3

7−3

= 3 4 5

Lost at Sea!

Help the ship reach a safe port. Track **QUESTRON** on the path that has the correct answers to the addition and subtraction problems in the stormy sea.

$10-5$

$9-2$

7

4

8

5

$7-4$

3

4

9

8

$10-2$

Finish

Beware of Bears!

Solve the "bear-y" easy word problem in each box.
Press **QUESTRON** on the correct answers.

There were

5

and

3

How many in all?

| 6 |
| 7 |
| 8 |

There were

8

then

3 ran away.

How many were left?

| 4 |
| 5 |
| 6 |

There were

7 HONEY

then

3 were eaten.

How many were left?

| 3 |
| 4 |
| 5 |

There were

9

5 had

How many didn't?

| 6 |
| 4 |
| 2 |

There were

4

The bears took 2

How many were left?

| 2 |
| 3 |
| 4 |

There were

6 and 4

How many in all?

| 8 |
| 9 |
| 10 |

There were

6 and 5

How many in all?

| 9 |
| 10 |
| 11 |

There were

10

then 8 were eaten.

How many were left?

| 5 |
| 3 |
| 2 |

Farmyard Pairs

Look at each pair of animals. Press **QUESTRON**
on the one that has the bigger number.

$3 + 2$

$4 - 1$

$5 + 3$

13

12

$6 + 4$

$4 + 9$

$5 + 6$

Parade of Animals

Which one comes first, second or third?
Is it the monkey, the giraffe or the bird?
Press **QUESTRON** on the answer that matches the picture.

first   second   third

first   second   third

sixth   seventh   eighth

fourth   fifth   sixth

fourth   fifth   sixth

sixth   seventh   eighth

fourth   fifth   sixth

first   second   third

Find the Facts

Three petals of each flower have addition or subtraction facts that match the answer shown in its centre. Press **QUESTRON** on each petal that has a correct answer.

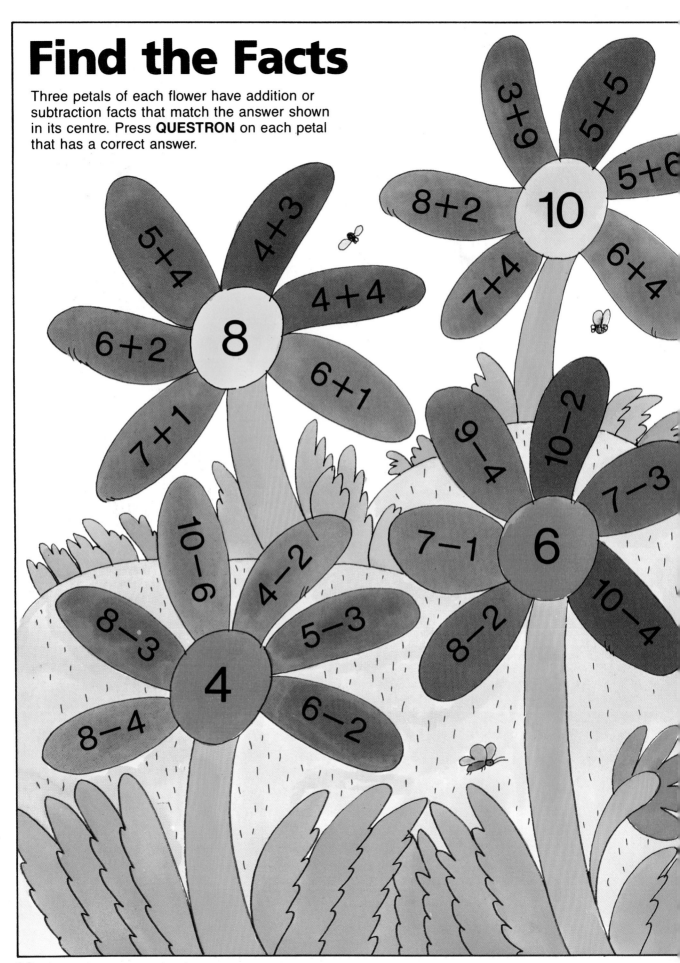

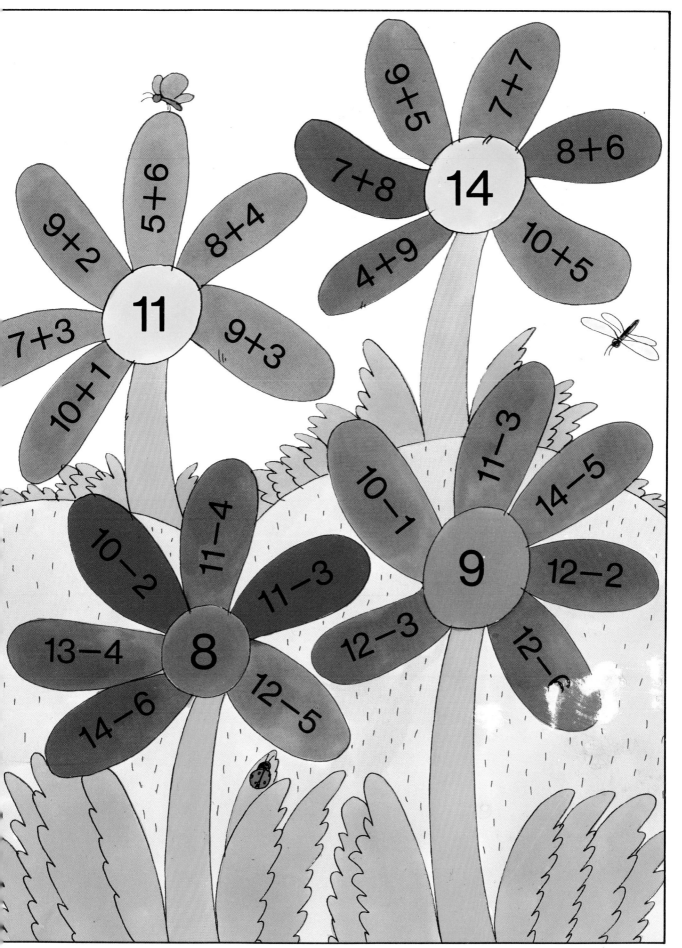

Monster Mazes

Read the directions for each maze and track **QUESTRON** on the correct numbers.

Follow the odd numbers.

2	52	16
11	13	15	31
22	30	14	9
3	1	7	25

Subtract 2.

17	15	16
16	19	13	12
8	14	11	10
6	12	9	7

Counting Can "Bee" Fun!

Counting by twos, by threes and by fives can help busy bees return to their hives. Read the directions over each bee and press **QUESTRON** on the correct numbers in each path.

"Begin here. Count by fives."

Searching for Shapes

Press **QUESTRON** on the circles.

Press **QUESTRON** on the squares.

Press **QUESTRON** on the triangles.

Press **QUESTRON** on the rectangles.

Fun with Fractions

Press **QUESTRON** on the number that matches the fraction shown in each picture.

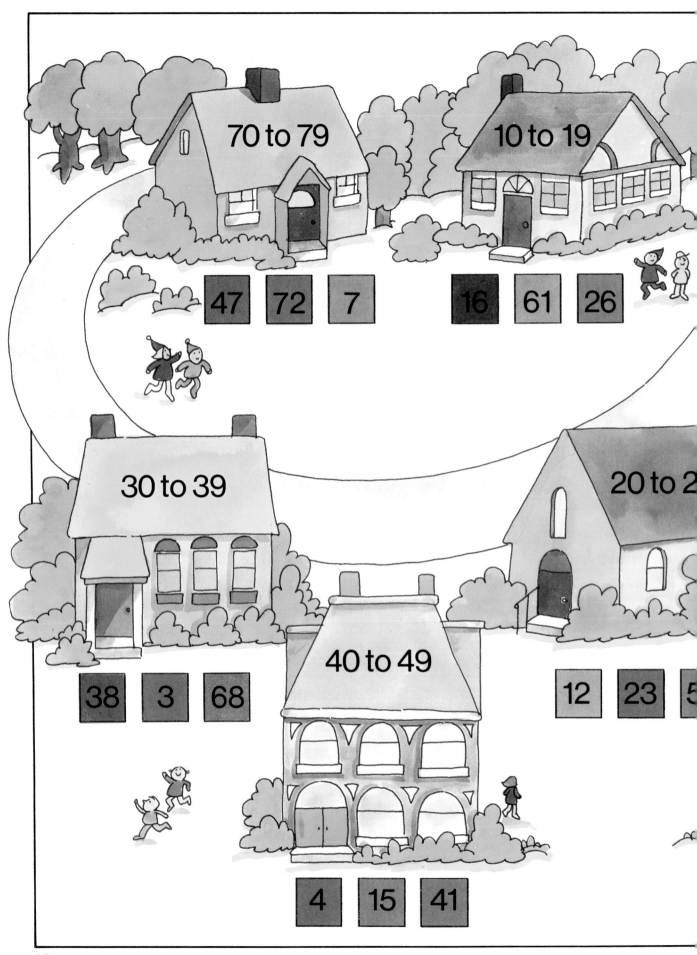

70 to 79

10 to 19

47 72 7

16 61 26

30 to 39

20 to 2

40 to 49

38 3 68

12 23 5

4 15 41

28

Number Places

Each building holds many numbers.
Press **QUESTRON** on the number
that belongs inside each one.

60 to 69

62 47 36

1 to 9

11 7 17

50 to 59

14 54 45

Mice are Nice!

Press **QUESTRON** on the balloon with the correct answer to each question.

Look, listen and join in the fun with

The Wee Sing range of cassettes and activity books are compiled by experienced preschool and early school teachers. The tapes include songs, games and rhymes. The books have the musical notes of the melody lines, so that children can have fun, sing along – and learn, too!

The Wee Sing and Colour series adds yet another dimension. The books not only contain the complete lyrics of the songs and rhymes – they also have line drawings of favourite characters to colour.

Wee Sing provides an hour of entertainment and music, and a songbook with no less than 64 pages. **Wee Sing and Colour** gives you some 30 minutes of songs, games and rhymes and a 48-page colouring book.

Wee Sing – early learning made fun.

Wee Sing

**Children's songs and fingerplays
Rhymes for play
Nursery rhymes and lullabies
Silly songs**

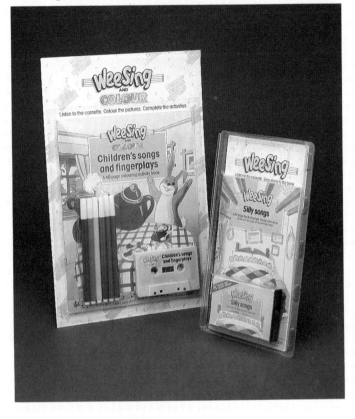

Wee Sing & Colour

**Children's songs and fingerplays
Musical games and rhymes
Christmas songs**

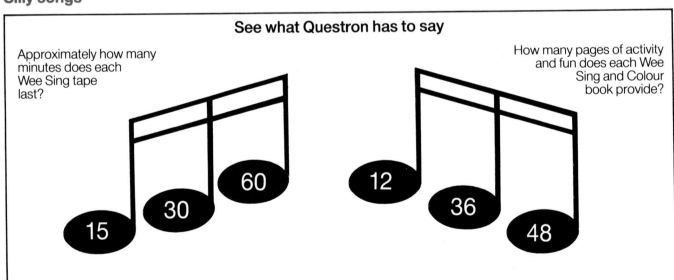

See what Questron has to say

Approximately how many minutes does each Wee Sing tape last?

15 30 60

How many pages of activity and fun does each Wee Sing and Colour book provide?

12 36 48

Another new product range from PSS – if you have difficulty in obtaining Wee Sing from your local stockist, please contact Price Stern Sloan Limited, John Clare House, The Avenue, Northampton NN1 5BT. Telephone (0604) 230344.